OWL
MOVES OUT
of the
FOREST

by Nikki Potts • illustrated by Maarten Lenoir

PICTURE WINDOW BOOKS
a capstone imprint

Mice. Squirrels. Bugs. Moles.

Lizards. Fish. Rabbits. Voles.

Owl spends each night
hunting for food.

Owl loves flying. Owl loves hunting.

Owl loves the trees
in his forest.

But everything is
always the same.
Owl is bored!

Owl flies across the ocean to look for a new, exciting home.

The ocean is larger than Owl thought. Owl is getting tired!

Owl dives into
the warm water.

There are bright corals
and colorful fish
everywhere.

Maybe Owl could live here.

WAIT!

WAIT!

WAIT!

Owl can't swim!

HELP!

The coral reef was not
a good home for Owl.

Owl shakes sand out
of his tail feathers.

He licks salt off his beak.

Then he takes off again.

Owl sees some
funny-looking trees.

He has always
wanted to live in a
funny-looking tree.

Owl spots a lion
in the distance.

But he knows the lion
can't reach him
at the top of the tree.

Suddenly, the branches shake.

A spotted face pokes
through the leaves.

A giraffe is eating Owl's nest!

The savanna is not a good home for Owl.

Owl has always
wanted to visit a
haunted house!

Maybe he will get a piece of candy while he's here too.

It's too scary here!

Owl doesn't WANT
to make a cemetery
his new home!

There is no place
more exciting than
New York City!

Watch out,
Big Apple.
Owl is here!

New York City is busy.

Owl has to fly around cars, people, and tall buildings.

WATCH OUT!

Owl wanted exciting.
This might be too exciting.

Turns out New
York City was
not a good home
for Owl either.

TAXI!

27

The forest might not
be exciting. It may
not be full of colorful
fish or bright lights or
funny-looking trees.

But it was the best
home for Owl all along.

ALL ABOUT GREAT HORNED OWLS

Female great horned owls are larger than males.

Soft feathers help the owls fly quietly.

Great horned owls can't move their big, yellow eyes. They have to turn their heads to see.

Strong, sharp talons help great horned owls hunt. They use their talons to grab prey.

Great horned owls hunt mostly at night.

ANIMAL PASSPORT

Name: Great Horned Owl

Type: bird

Habitat: North America and South America

Diet: meat

Height: up to 25 inches (63.5 centimeters); up to 4.8 foot (1.5 meters) wingspan

Weight: up to 5.5 pounds (2.5 kilograms)

Lifespan: 5 to 15 years

Favorite activity: hunting mice

BOOKS IN THIS SERIES

Habitat Hunter is published by Picture Window Books, an imprint of Capstone.
1710 Roe Crest Drive
North Mankato, Minnesota 56003
www.capstonepub.com

Library of Congress Cataloging-in-Publication Data is available on the Library of Congress website.
ISBN: 978-1-9771-1424-2 (library binding)
ISBN: 978-1-9771-2022-9 (paperback)
ISBN: 978-1-9771-1430-3 (eBook PDF)

Summary: Owl is bored with its habitat! Follow Owl as it tries out different places to live. Which habitat will make the best home for Owl?

Image Credits
Shutterstock: 2630ben, 14, Alexander Kalina, cover, CK Foto, 28-29, Creaturart Images, 20-21, Curioso, 26-27, Danita Delmont, 16-17, dibrova, 22-23, Ewa Studio, 7, Fanfo, 4-5, GaudiLab, 24-25, Graeme Shannon, 12-13, Ian Scott, 8-9, Martin Maun, 6, MH STOCK, 10-11, Nejron Photo, 14-15, Peyker, cover, Razvan Ionut Dragomirescu, 18-19, Tony Morn, 31, Triff, 2-3, Vector8DIY, backcover

Artistic Elements: pingebat, Valeriya_Dor

Editorial Credits
Editor: Mari Bolte; Designer: Kayla Rossow; Media Researcher: Kelly Garvin; Production Specialist: Tori Abraham

All internet sites appearing in back matter were available and accurate when this book was sent to press.